WRITTEN BY
JEFF LUCAS
JAN/FEB 2017

CW01651931

EVERY DAY

Table Talk

Published 2016 by CWR, Waverley Abbey House, Waverley Lane, Farnham, Surrey GU9 8EP, UK
Tel: 01252 784700 Email: mail@cwr.org.uk Registered Charity No. 294387
Registered Limited Company No. 1990308
Front cover image: Stocksy/Jill Chen
Concept development, editing, design and production by CWR.
Printed in the UK by Linney Print.

CWR

MIX
Paper from responsible sources
FSC
www.fsc.org
FSC® C015900

HOW TO GET THE BEST OUT OF *LIFE EVERY DAY*

HERE ARE A FEW SUGGESTIONS:

- Ideally, carve out a regular time and place each day, with as few distractions as possible. Ask God what He has to say to you.

- Read the Bible passages suggested in the 'READ' references. (As tempting as it is, try not to skip the Bible reading and get straight into the notes.)

- The 'FOCUS' reference then gives you one or two verses to look at in more detail. Consider what the reading is saying to you and what challenges that may bring.

- Each day's comments are part of an overall theme. Try to recall what you read the previous day so that you maintain a sense of continuity.

- Spend time thinking about how to apply what God has said to you. Ask Him to help you do this.

- Pray the prayer at the end as if it were your own. Perhaps add your own prayer in response to what you have read and been thinking about.

Join in the conversation on Facebook
www.facebook.com/jefflucasuk

READ:
Luke 15:1–2 //
Colossians 3:17

Weekend

A good idea gone bad

It's a truth that we'd all do well to embrace: all of life is to be an act of worship. Worship is not just a weekend event, a series of songs sung, or liturgy shared. We're called to live all of our lives before God, doing whatever we do in His name. Now that's a great resolution for the new year.

But the best ideas can be corrupted. In Jesus' day, the Pharisees wanted every meal to be like an act of worship in the Temple, and were described by some scholars as 'a table fellowship sect'. But fanaticism crouches at the door of commitment and passion. They had 229 texts of regulations about table fellowship, covering minute details. All food had to have been subject to tithing, and was carefully prepared with ritual hand washings. One could not share a meal with anyone who might 'defile' the proceedings. So practices that were intended to express commitment to holiness were now being used to exclude. And Jesus refused to comply with those man-made rules, and was heavily criticised because of it. Let's know the difference between devotion and fanaticism.

To ponder: What is the difference between commitment and fanaticism?

Jesus refused to comply

MON 02 JAN

The sinner classes

READ:
Matthew 9:11–13
Romans 3:21–24

FOCUS
'When the Pharisees saw this, they asked his disciples, "Why does your teacher eat with tax collectors and sinners?"' (Matt. 9:11)

Jesus was criticised, as we saw yesterday, for eating with 'sinners'. But that doesn't just mean that He was dining with people of bad reputation. He sat down to eat with those who had been designated specifically as untrustworthy outcasts. These were those who practised one of the 'seven despised trades', including tax collectors, barbers, tanners and shepherds, or who were considered guilty of flagrant immorality, such as prostitutes, adulterers, gamblers and murderers. Also, those who did not observe the law according to the Pharisees' understanding of it were designated as sinners too. And then of course all Gentiles were considered to be sinners and outsiders as well (Mark 14:41; Gal. 2:15).

Notice that it is said that Jesus was friends with '*tax collectors* and sinners'. The tax gatherers were a group especially singled out for a mention (more on that later). It was believed that if a tax collector entered any house, the food and the entire house were rendered unclean. Some even taught that repentance was completely impossible for them. They were seen as collaborators with the occupying forces, lackeys of Rome, and a threat to the cohesion of the community's goal of holiness. No wonder there was such conflict when some of them became Jesus' friends.

Before we think about this any further, let's ask: are there people groups or individuals that we consider to be beyond God's grace? In the name of holiness, it's possible for us to become exclusive too.

Prayer: Help me never to dismiss anyone as being beyond Your grace, Lord. You save sinners – like me. Amen.

Risky grace

● TUES 03 JAN

READ:
Matthew 22:1–14
Isaiah 55:1–2

FOCUS
'Jesus spoke to them again in parables, saying: "The kingdom of heaven is like a king who prepared a wedding banquet for his son."' (Matt. 22:1–2)

In Jesus' day, sharing a meal was considered an act of intimacy and fellowship; to offer hospitality was to give honour and trusting acceptance. Refusing to share a meal, conversely, signalled rejection and disapproval.

But there were political implications to table fellowship. It was a symbol to a people whose nation was occupied by a hated force, the Romans. The Pharisees saw the preservation of the eating traditions as a vital part of maintaining Jewish culture, an important element of their unity. And, as we noted yesterday, shared meals were an expression of holiness. The Pharisees believed that if they could nudge people back to greater faithfulness to God (expressed through keeping all their intricate rules) then liberation from oppression would come. So Jesus' eating with sinners would have been viewed as an act of betrayal, both to the nation and to God.

In other words, eating with sinners was incredibly risky. So why take the risk?

Jesus was demonstrating a picture of the kingdom of God, where the outsiders are in, where the proud are dismissed and the humble are exalted. But He was also showing tenderness and care for hurting people who felt like social pariahs. In the words of the Anglican Communion Service, 'he touched untouchables with love and washed the guilty clean'.*

I'd like to take the risk and navigate misunderstandings in order to include more people in the kingdom banquet. Let's go 'out of our way' to extend grace.

tenderness and care for hurting people

Prayer: Use me as an agent of grace, of kindness, of welcome today, living God. Amen.

*Church of England, *Common Worship: Holy Communion Order One Booklet* (Norwich: Church House Publishing, 2000)

● WED 04 JAN

Loving the hated

READ:
Matthew 5:43–48
Luke 6:36–42

FOCUS
'But I tell you, love your enemies and pray for those who persecute you, that you may be children of your Father in heaven.' (Matt. 5:44–45)

We've already seen that Jesus modelled inclusion, bringing people from the outside in. But His dining habits show us that God wants us to go further; He wants us to love people that others hate. Jesus' dining with a despised tax collector shows that, but His story about the 'good' Samaritan takes it further. Samaritans were viewed as unclean heretics. Yet in the story, Jesus declares this enemy of Israel to be 'good', because of his caring compassionate attitude.

Those who listened to Jesus' teaching would have entirely expected the priest and the Levite to 'pass by on the other side', as to be within four cubits of a dying or dead person would render one unclean. Even allowing your shadow to pass over the corpse, or passing under the shadow of a rock that overhung a corpse, would also create uncleanness.* A Jew was only required to stop and help a fellow Jew if they were in need of aid, which would have meant that the priest and Levite would have had to take a risk. The Pharisaic thinking of the day would have applauded their passing by, not taking the 'risk' of defilement. But Jesus challenged that thinking, teaching that it is better to take chances on the side of compassion than stay in the safety of personal 'cleanliness'. In the same way, the father in the Prodigal story had compassion on his son (Luke 15:20).

Who is hated in our culture? Let's think about that, and ask if there are ways to extend kindness to those who only experience hostility and rejection.

Who is hated in our culture?

Prayer: Lord, show me where there is hatred in me and, by Your Spirit, replace it with love. Amen.

*J. Duncan M. Derrett, *Law in the New Testament* (Eugene, Oregon: Wipf and Stock, 2005) pp208–227

CWR MINISTRY EVENTS

Please pray for the team

DATE	EVENT	PLACE	PRESENTER(S)
6 Jan	BA Counselling Year 1 resumes	Pilgrim Hall	Waverley Abbey College team
13 Jan	BA Counselling Year 3 resumes	PH	Waverley Abbey College team
13 Jan	MA Counselling Year 1 resumes	Waverley Abbey House	Waverley Abbey College team
16 Jan	BA Counselling Year 4 resumes	PH	Waverley Abbey College team
20 Jan	BA Counselling Year 2 resumes	PH	Waverley Abbey College team
20 Jan	MA Relational Counselling and Psychotherapy resumes	WAH	Waverley Abbey College team
23–27 Jan	January Country Break	PH	Ewart Helyar and Pilgrim Hall team
26 Jan	Refreshing Your Spiritual Life	WAH	Andy Peck
26 Jan	MA Counselling Year 2 resumes	WAH	Waverley Abbey College team
4 Feb	Winter Glory Conference	Kettering Conference Centre	Lynette Brooks and Rosalyn Derges
9 Feb	Structuring Pastoral Care	WAH	Andy Peck
21 Feb	Prayer Breakfast	PH	Pilgrim Hall team
23 Feb	Sharing Jesus	WAH	Andy Peck

We would also appreciate prayer for our ongoing ministry in Singapore and Cambodia, as well as the many regional events that we are embarking on this year.

For further information and a full list of CWR's courses, seminars and events, call **+44 (0)1252 784719** or visit **www.cwr.org.uk/courses**

You can also download our free Prayer Track, which includes daily prayers, from **www.cwr.org.uk/free-resources**

THURS 05 JAN

'Toxic' holiness

READ:
Mark 5:1–20
1 Peter 1:13–16

FOCUS
'He shouted at the top of his voice, "What do you want with me, Jesus, Son of the Most High God?"' (Mark 5:7)

It's an idea that has plagued the people of God throughout the ages: that, to be truly holy, you have to separate yourself from the rest of the world. When I became a Christian, I abandoned my non-Christian friends and disappeared into the warm confines of the Church, fearing that association would cause contamination.

But Jesus challenged the popular ideas about holiness by sharing meals with 'sinners'. He replaced these ideas with an alternative vision. He was showing that authentic holiness is a powerful, positive force that can change those who come into contact with it. Holiness does not need to be cloistered. Far from being fragile, it is able to bring wholeness where there is brokenness, and scatter the forces of darkness. The leper does not make Jesus unclean, but rather is cleansed by Him (Mark 1:40–45). The possessed Gerasene man was unclean for so many reasons (he lived among tombs, in Gentile territory, near swine, and was possessed by an unclean spirit). Yet he is cleansed by the power of Jesus' holy presence. The wonderful truth of the clean hallowing the unclean is continued in Paul's thinking about the sanctifying effect of the Christian (1 Cor. 7:12–14).

If we've been living with a set of people who commonly share destructive lifestyle habits, it may well be sensible to break ties with them when we come to Christ. But let's see if we can live with greater effect, rather than being affected. If we take away the salt, then the rot will set in.

holiness is a powerful, positive force

Prayer: Help me to live a life that is salt and light today, Lord God. Amen.

Responding to criticism

FRI 06 JAN

READ:
1 Peter 2:23
John 6:41–43

FOCUS
'When they hurled their insults at him, he did not retaliate; when he suffered, he made no threats.' (1 Pet. 2:23)

Nobody likes to be criticised. It is especially hard when the criticism is unwarranted, or comes from those who care little about us (or even the issue that they're raising) but only want to hurt. Jesus dealt with continuous criticism throughout His ministry, but had an amazing ability to respond to it well. Some of us get paralysed by criticism. Not only do we find it devastating, but we go to inappropriate lengths to avoid it, and worry constantly about what other people think about us. Or we may go to the other extreme and seem quite impervious to the opinions of others. That can lead to big trouble too. Critics can help us because they can be absolutely right, and their words might prevent us from blundering into disaster.

When criticised, Jesus usually explained His actions but carried on doing what He knew was right. When attacked for His eating habits, Jesus insisted that those excluded by religion (like Zacchaeus the tax collector) could be part of God's people as 'a son of Abraham' (Luke 19:7–10).

Jesus saw the 'sinners' as being like sick people in need of help and health, with Him as the doctor (Mark 2:15–17), and table fellowship was to be part of the restorative process. And He refused to play religious games or submit to what some saw as orthodoxy.

Let's hear our critics, because they may be our greatest allies, even if their tone is hurtful. But in hearing them, let's not become slaves to them.

Prayer: When unwelcome words come, help me to learn from them, but not be controlled by them. Help me to do what is right in Your sight, Lord. Amen.

07/08 JAN

Weekend

READ:

Luke 5:27–32 //
Romans 12:1–2

Revolution

Having a meal with Jesus brought more than a few revisions in behaviour for Levi. He got a brand-new life, a new identity, and a new name. Just as Simon became Peter, so Levi became Matthew, which means 'gift of God', an ironic name for a man who was notorious for grabbing rather than giving.

And the giving started immediately. Matthew threw a lavish banquet in Jesus' honour; an expensive undertaking, particularly for a man who was turning his back on his lucrative franchise. Unlike the fishermen in Jesus' team, Levi's walking away from his tarnished profession was irreversible. This was a huge step of faith.

Money can ensnare us, driving us to exploit and oppress. The old Levi had squandered his reputation and social status in his relentless pursuit of material gain. But when Jesus came by, a new attitude was birthed, an almost childlike attitude of faith and trust.

Not only can we be different, but we can become precisely the opposite of what we have been, through the work of the Spirit of God in us. We are not sentenced to sameness.

To ponder: How would you like to be radically different from what and who you are now?

We are not sentenced to sameness

CWR
Helping you live life God's way
...through uniting and equipping the Church

Church programmes are one of the main heartbeats of CWR. For more than five decades we have served the Church with teaching and inspiring resources, underpinned by God's Word. In recent years we have developed our church programmes, which unite and strengthen churches as they learn and grow together in their walk with God. These programmes cover topics from pastoral care to exploring personal identity, and are all based on biblical teaching.

Paraclesis: Journeying Together – a six-week series that provides a fresh perspective on caring for one another through life's struggles. Teaching the whole church to come alongside people. **www.paraclesis.org.uk**

40 Days with Jesus – a six-week series that explores the accounts of the risen Jesus and the impact He has on those He encounters in the 40 days between Easter and Pentecost. **www.40days.info**

Transformed Life – a seven-week series that uses Ephesians 1–3 to explore questions about identity, purpose and belonging. **www.transformed-life.info**

And introducing **Transformed Living** – new to 2017, a seven-week series for the whole church, offering dynamic and practical teaching from Ephesians 4–6. **www.transformed-living.info**

● MON 09 JAN

READ:
Luke 5:27–32
1 Corinthians 1:26–30

FOCUS
'After this, Jesus went out and saw a tax collector by the name of Levi sitting at his tax booth.' (Luke 5:27)

An unlikely candidate

It's an issue that has rightly created huge anger in our nation, as short-term lending companies charge staggering rates of interest, exploiting those who are already struggling to make ends meet. As we look more closely at the first of Luke's meals, it's important to reaffirm just how unlikely it was that Levi would either share a meal with Jesus or join His team. Levi owned a tax franchise, having done a deal with the Roman authorities – a step that meant that he was viewed as a traitor to the Jewish nation, profiting from the national tragedy of Roman occupation. The taxmen could charge pretty much anything they liked, paying the government their share and then skimming a tidy profit for themselves. And their power was immense, enabling them to stop any traveller and demand taxes and tolls from them. If they couldn't pay, the tax official would become a short-term lender, offering bridging finance at outrageous rates of interest. Greed is nothing new! Jewish tax collectors were excommunicated from the synagogues and disqualified from being witnesses in the law courts. But Levi was to become Matthew, one of the twelve disciples and the writer of the first Gospel, a witness to Christ.

In choosing Levi/Matthew, Jesus was sending a clear signal that absolutely everything is different in His kingdom, and that everyone can experience the revolution that we considered yesterday. No preconditions apply, no prejudice, no list of exclusions. Everyone.

No preconditions apply

Prayer: Lord, help me to pray and believe for those who seem unlikely to respond to Your love. Amen.

It was a good look

TUES 10 JAN

READ:
Luke 5:27
Psalm 33:12–15

FOCUS
'After this, Jesus went out and saw a tax collector by the name of Levi sitting at his tax booth.' (Luke 5:27)

Imagine it. None other than Jesus is walking by. Suddenly, He turns in His tracks, and you realise that He is walking towards you. And then He stops, says nothing, but just looks at you. The word that Luke uses to describe Jesus seeing Levi suggests that Jesus took a long look. But it seems that this was not a stare of interrogation, or a look that intimidated. It was a good look, literally, prompting Levi to make the cataclysmic decision to abandon his lucrative but crooked career to become a full-time follower of this strange, wonderful rabbi named Jesus.

Friedrich Nietzsche, famous for his 'death of God' philosophy, hated the idea of being seen by God. The son of a Lutheran minister, Nietzsche complained that God 'saw with eyes that saw everything; he saw man's depths ... all his concealed disgrace and ugliness ... he crawled into my dirtiest nooks. This most curious ... one had to die.'* Tragically, Nietzsche interpreted God's interest as intrusion, and thought that God saw only a sinful heart, instead of the heart of someone that He greatly loved. And that misunderstanding drove him to loathe God, and try to assassinate Him with his pen.

How might Jesus look at us? Perhaps instinctively we fear that He might focus on our shortcomings and sins with a cold, sterile stare. Perhaps we need to ponder the truth that Jesus sees us exactly as we are, but His look is one of love, of joy, of grace. And the look is not a cursory glance, but one of intense interest and care.

Prayer: Lord, I am grateful that when You look my way there is tenderness and love in Your eyes. Amen.

*Friedrich Nietzsche, translated by Walter Kaufmann, *The Portable Nietzsche* (New York, New York: Penguin, 1994) p378

WED 11 JAN

An event worth celebrating

READ:
Luke 5:27–29
Luke 15:8–10

FOCUS
'Then Levi held a great banquet for Jesus at his house, and a large crowd of tax collectors and others were eating with them.'
(Luke 5:29)

Yesterday, I had the joy of hosting a radio conversation with an old friend, George Verwer, the founder of Operation Mobilisation. His story, documented in a book and a new film published by CWR, is well worth a read. From his earliest days, he has been passionate about sharing the good news of Jesus. In his latter years, he has focused more on grace, admitting that he had an unhealthy tendency towards legalism early in his journey. George shared his belief that now is the greatest time in the history of the Christian Church; people are turning to Christ in droves all around the world. This news may not make the headlines, but it's true.

Ending our conversation, I felt exhilarated and encouraged, not just by George's wonderful personality but by the amazing news that each and every day there are people choosing to follow Jesus. That fact should stir our hearts. A new birth has taken place. Old patterns of living have been interrupted, and now another citizen of the kingdom of heaven is on planet Earth. In Levi's case, his conversion led to a huge party.

When people decide to follow Jesus, let's celebrate. Let them know that theirs is the most wonderful decision of their entire life, a more significant choice even than getting married, having children, or getting to that much hoped-for career opportunity. Eternity is different. Peace with God has been established. New life has come. The angels in heaven are partying. Our response should surely mirror theirs.

The angels in heaven are partying

Prayer: I praise You, mighty God, for the great work that You are doing across the earth. May I truly celebrate when others come to know You. Amen.

Sharing our story

● THURS 12 JAN

READ:
Luke 5:27–29
Luke 8:26–39

FOCUS
'Then Levi held a great banquet for Jesus at his house, and a large crowd of tax collectors and others were eating with them.'
(Luke 5:29)

I've talked about this before, because it's a subject close to my heart, and one that causes me great concern. Whatever happened to evangelism? Years ago, when I became a Christian, the Church was very intentional about sharing Jesus, to the point that it could become mechanical and contrived. There was very little social engagement from the evangelical wing of the Church back then: we were good at news, but not so good at living it out. This was a deficiency, as we'll see tomorrow, because God's heart of compassion demands our engagement with social justice.

But I wonder if we have overreacted, increasingly giving ourselves to wonderful projects and initiatives that serve our communities, but failing to share the reason for our efforts. We need to say we have been won by the love of Christ, a love we want to share.

Levi's conversion was a very public affair. The party that he threw was surely not only to honour Jesus, but to share with his community the news that his old life was over and he was beginning anew. Nobody was left in any doubt: Levi was a new man. And the demonised man that encountered Jesus was given this command: 'Return home and tell how much God has done for you' (Luke 8:39).

I don't want to go back to the old days of breathlessly blurting out evangelistic monologues. But I do want to be ready to share the greatest news available to humanity, as I am ready to give a reason for the hope that I have in Jesus (1 Pet. 3:15–16).

Prayer: I am available today, Lord, to share the good news about You, and what You have done for me. Guide my steps. Amen.

● FRI 13 JAN

READ:
Matthew 9:9–13
Hosea 6:1–6

FOCUS
'But go and learn what this means: "I desire mercy, not sacrifice."' *(Matt. 9:13)*

Mercy not sacrifice

Perhaps we've all met them: people who are incredibly intense about matters of faith and religious practice, but who are just not very nice, and don't demonstrate a lot of love. Instead of being welcoming and friendly, they seem to delight in telling people that God doesn't like them. The Pharisees exemplified this attitude.

Let's turn away from the account from Luke just for a moment, and go to Matthew's Gospel, where he describes Levi's conversion in the third person (a strange thing to do, as Levi and Matthew were one and the same). In his account, Matthew includes the truth that Luke affirms – that Jesus has not come for the healthy, but for the sick. He expands this by remembering that Jesus quoted from Hosea, the prophet who had called Israel away from empty ritual to a true heart of compassion for the poor.

Religiously fastidious behaviour means nothing to God. He's looking for a heart that cares for the bruised and the broken. And we can surely extend that truth further to the simple principle that those who truly love God will truly love people – a reality that John hammers home in his epistles: 'Whoever claims to love God yet hates a brother or sister is a liar' (1 John 4:20).

We can easily fool ourselves into believing that our attendance at worship, our study of Scripture and our commitment to personal holiness are all God wants. But He is looking for people who love Him, and people who will love people.

He is looking for... people who will love people

Prayer: Help me to care about what You care about, Father, and live a life that expresses that heart. Amen.

READ:

Luke 13:31–32 //
John 3:1–21

Weekend

Pharisaic about Pharisees

Prejudice can crouch in the most unusual places.

I hate legalism, and get upset when faith is complicated by picky people who insist that others follow rules and regulations that have nothing to do with Scripture. But I recently discovered an uncomfortable truth about myself: I have become pharisaic about people that I perceive are acting like Pharisees. I'll be quick to offer grace to those who fail, but become impatient with those whom I write off as 'religious'. The former can have a humility that the latter lack!

We tend to think of the Pharisees as the consistent 'bad guys' in the Gospel stories, and we instinctively boo and hiss them every time they appear. But Jesus did not dine only with sinners, but with those who tended to think of themselves as saints too. Some Pharisees tried to help Jesus, warning Him about Herod. And, as we'll see this week, Jesus spent time socially with some Pharisees. Jesus didn't write the Pharisees off, but gave at least one of them the opportunity to discuss faith with Him, as the story of Nicodemus shows. Know anyone who seems pharisaic? Maybe it's time to invite them for lunch.

To ponder: Ask God to show you if you have any 'subtle' prejudices.

Jesus did not dine only with sinners

In Simon's house

● MON 16 JAN

READ:
Luke 7:36–50
1 Peter 4:8

FOCUS
'I came into your house. You did not give me any water for my feet, but she wet my feet with her tears and wiped them with her hair.' (Luke 7:44)

It's a trait in me that I'm desperately trying to work on, and more significantly it's what I'm asking God to change: I can be irritated by behaviour patterns that are relatively insignificant, like ingratitude. I think I'm a generous person, but if I don't feel appreciated, or get a hint that my generosity is being presumed upon (or worse still, I'm being manipulated), I get upset. And then there are times when I can make an issue over something that really isn't very important, but I'mcompelled to sort it out. I forget that not everything needs resolution, and that love 'covers a multitude of sins'. Sometimes we just need to move on, resisting the urge to correct every fault that we see.

When Jesus went to Simon the Pharisee's house, He was treated with disrespect that was scandalous in the culture of the day. His Pharisee host ignored the basic customs of welcome and honour, implying that he didn't value Jesus as a person, but only wanted to gawk at what he saw as an amusing new celebrity. This would have been highly hurtful and embarrassing. But it was only after the Pharisee started to criticise the actions of the 'sinful' woman that Jesus raised the issue of Simon's neglectful behaviour. Jesus could have acted out of offence, but instead chose to keep quiet until there was an opportunity for a redemptive conversation.

Let's not make an issue out of every issue, otherwise we will hurt unnecessarily, and spend our lives in conflict.

Prayer: Help me to know when to speak, when to confront, and when to just leave well alone, Lord. Amen.

● TUES 17 JAN

Scandalous worship

READ:
Luke 7:36–50
John 4:1–24

FOCUS
'As she stood behind him at his feet weeping, she began to wet his feet with her tears. Then she wiped them with her hair, kissed them and poured perfume on them.' (Luke 7:38)

Worship has become something of a consumer product. A hilarious spoof report appeared on the internet recently, describing a 'calamity' in a large, youthful church, where people missed the presence of the Holy Spirit because the smoke machine had broken down. This piece made the point that worship can become a theatrical event, where famous worship leaders preside over what seems more like a concert than an expression of worship. And then we have our 'favourite' worship songs, and sadly, often the greatest source of conflict in local churches is the style of worship.

To Jesus, worship was simple even when it was fragile, as was the case with the 'sinful woman'. Luke doesn't attempt to hide her reputation – most likely as a prostitute – and he doesn't try to shield us from what must have seemed like an act that was somewhat erotic. First, for her to let her hair down was shocking (it has been likened to a woman going topless). And then her tender caressing of Jesus' feet must have seemed outrageous. It's possible that she responded to Jesus this way because she had been so engrained with the idea that the only way to respond to a man was with touch. But Jesus saw past the fragilities in her worship, and instead of rebuking her and creating distance, He commended her. Sometimes our offerings of worship are amateurish, off-key, and mingled with mixed motives. But we can bring them to Jesus anyway, who accepts our broken attempts with gladness.

Jesus... accepts our broken attempts with gladness

Prayer: Lord, help me to be a worshipper in spirit and in truth, worshipping You, not worshipping worship. Amen.

A slur

WED 18 JAN

READ:
Luke 7:36–50
Luke 15:11–32

FOCUS
'When the Pharisee ... saw this, he said to himself, "If this man were a prophet, he would know who is touching him and what kind of woman she is – that she is a sinner."' (Luke 7:39)

When Jesus allowed the 'sinful' woman to touch Him, He was obviously taking a huge risk. People could assume the wrong thing, and they did. There must have been some prior interaction between Jesus and the woman on an earlier occasion, because Jesus explains that her devotion to Him was a grateful response to the news that she had been forgiven. In some earlier unrecorded episode, He must have met her and offered forgiveness.

But when the host of the meal commented to himself on what was happening, the word for 'touched' that he used is often used in a sexual context, usually for sexual intercourse. The Pharisee, while obviously not suggesting that the woman was trying to make love to Jesus, infers that there is impurity in her action, and in a way that shouldn't surprise us because of her reputation. Just as the elder brother insists that the returning prodigal has squandered the family wealth with prostitutes (the first mention of prostitution in the story) so the Pharisee immediately jumps to the worst conclusion.

It's too tempting to label people with the phrase 'they always', and conclude that they are behaving badly now because they've behaved badly in the past. And, as this happened in the context of a worshipful moment, it's worth saying that we can do that when someone expresses themselves in worship in a way that is unusual: that they are strange, or attention-seeking. Without being naive, let's try to believe the best, and not the worst.

Prayer: Save me from unhelpful speculation about the sins of others, gracious God. Amen.

THURS 19 JAN

Basic Christianity

READ:
Luke 7:36–50
1 John 1:5–10

FOCUS
'Therefore, I tell you, her many sins have been forgiven – as her great love has shown.' (Luke 7:47)

It caused more than a stir. A well-known American politician, who claimed to be a Christian, was asked about his faith. Worryingly, he couldn't think of a single Bible verse when asked what his most treasured Scripture passage was. But of greater concern was his affirmation that he had never once asked God to forgive him.

Being forgiven is the basis, the foundational starting point, for beginning the Christian life. Discipleship starts with the recognition that we have need of Jesus. He comes not as an adviser, emergency first responder or guide, but as the Saviour who endured the cross in order to save us from our sins. That recognition calls us to bow the knee in submission to Christ, not just extend a handshake of casual acknowledgment of His existence.

Jesus began His ministry by calling people to repent. As we've seen before in these *Life Every Day* notes, repentance speaks of a complete change of mind. It is not just recognition of and sorrow for our sin, but it does include that. Elsewhere, John makes it clear that if we say we have no sin (which implies that we think we don't need forgiveness) we deceive ourselves, and the truth is not in us.

And so a Christian who has never asked for forgiveness is surely no Christian at all. Even a so-called 'sinful woman' knew that total forgiveness is available.

Prayer: I need You, Lord: Your mercy, Your strength, Your direction, but also You. Amen.

Managing God and success

FRI 20 JAN

READ:
Luke 9:1–12
Deuteronomy 8:10–18

FOCUS
'Late in the afternoon the Twelve came to him and said, "Send the crowd away so they can go to the surrounding villages and countryside and find food and lodging"' (Luke 9:12)

As we turn now to the very public event that was the feeding of the 5,000, consider the context of the episode. The disciples had been sent out on totally faith-based mission, where they were told to take nothing in terms of supplies, but just to trust God for provision. They experienced spectacular success, which included supernatural healings.

But now, fresh from their heady adventure, they are invited to join Jesus as He heads for some welcome peace and quiet. The crowds find out though, and follow Him. Despite the interruption, Jesus welcomes them and teaches them. And when the time gets to around 4.30pm (it would get dark at around 6pm at that time of the year), the disciples suggest that Jesus dismisses the crowd so that everyone could get something to eat. Those who suggest there was no miracle of multiplication here, or that the little boy sharing his lunch prompted everyone to share theirs, are missing the point: if everyone had food, there would be no need to send them away! But the disciples, armed with what they have gained from their successful preaching tour, are now trying to manage Jesus.

Success, especially when it brings power, can be ruinous. A taste of success can change a person. They start to act with a sense of entitlement, and believe that their way is the only way. And they can even begin to think that God is at their beck and call. May you be graced with success, and blessed with grace to survive it.

A taste of success can change a person

Prayer: When I experience power or success, help me to remember You, my source, and submit to You, Lord. Amen.

Weekend

READ:
Luke 9:1–13 //
Mark 16:20

Partnership

Prayer. I've confessed frequently that not only am I not terribly good at it (my mind drifts, and I often fall asleep), but there have been times when I have faced an awkward question: what's the point of it? It's not that I don't believe that God is mighty and powerful, but if that is true, then why does He need me to ask Him to do things? And, if He is all-knowing, then He is very well aware of the need, so why do I apparently need to inform Him?

Surely the only answer to this is that God invites His people into partnership with Him, and has determined that what He does on the earth will be in active cooperation with His people. Just as God did nothing without telling Moses, so He calls us to be His confidants in His purposes. So when the disciples tell Jesus what to do about a catering crisis, He tries to nudge them into action with the invitation, 'You give them something to eat' (Luke 9:13). Remember, they have just returned from a faith-based mission. Now surely He wants them to use that faith in this situation of need. We're partners with God.

To ponder: Have you ever prayed that God would act, but He was calling you to become the answer to your own prayers?

God invites His people into partnership

MON 23 JAN

The big story continues

READ:
Luke 9:1–13
2 Kings 4:42–44

FOCUS
'He replied, "You give them something to eat."' (Luke 9:13)

As we read about the miracle of the feeding of the 5,000, perhaps there are other Bible stories that come to mind. In the story of Elisha, there was a time when a hundred men were fed with just twenty loaves of bread. In that episode, similar language is used, as Elisha's servant presents the dilemma to his boss (that there isn't enough to go around). Elisha says, 'Give it to them to eat.' And just as in the feeding of the 5,000, there was food left over too.

The 5,000 feeding is also pre-shadowed by Moses and the feeding of the Israelites in the wilderness, when manna came down from heaven. Luke wants us to know that the source of all provision, and the One who eternally pre-existed when both Moses and Elisha lived, was now alive as a man in Israel. And the stories are linked, all as part of the unfolding drama of God's interaction with planet Earth.

The story continues today, and we are part of it. Our partnership with God is not just about bringing people to our churches, or even making a difference in serving our communities, but is nothing less than participation in the Creator God's plan for the world that He loves. Next time we feel tired of serving, or we're tempted to take an easier road that doesn't call for obedience to what we know is right, let's remember that discipleship is not just about us living better lives. It is giving our unique contribution in the drama that included Moses, Elisha, Jesus, and now us.

Prayer: Thank You, Father, for the privilege that I, together with the people of God everywhere, am part of Your big story. Amen.

Faith for today

TUES 24 JAN

READ:
Luke 9:10–17
Isaiah 43:18–19

FOCUS
'They answered, "We have only five loaves of bread and two fish – unless we go and buy food for all this crowd."' (Luke 9:13)

In the Gospels, Jesus' disciples are not portrayed as clever, intuitive people, quick to understand His teaching. Theirs was a world-changing mission; Jesus would entrust them with the responsibility of taking the good news planet-wide. But they often completely misunderstood His instructions, like here, where they think He is asking them to go shopping rather than have faith for a multiplication miracle. It is quite encouraging, really!

Let's remind ourselves that they had just returned from a successful mission, where they had demonstrated faith for both provision and supernatural healing. But yesterday's steps of faith don't guarantee that we will trust God or rightly interpret what He says to us today.

I can think of faith steps that my family and I have taken in bygone years. As a young pastor, I was told that it was impossible to obtain a piece of land for a church building. Our little congregation marched around the plot that we'd spotted, and asked God to give it to us. A few days later, the local council reversed their decision and approved our application. And then there was the time when we returned from America to live in the UK, with only temporary housing and a guarantee of just £4,000 per year to live on. We trusted God, and He supplied. But those faith steps are now just part of my history, and while I am strengthened as I recall them, I'm challenged by this: will I put my faith in God throughout the challenges and demands that are current today?

Prayer: You have called me into partnership with You today, Lord. What can we do together? Amen.

We trusted God, and He supplied

● WED 25 JAN

An invisible boundary

READ:
Luke 10:38–42
Galatians 3:26–29

FOCUS
'Jesus … came to a village where a woman named Martha opened her home to him. She had a sister called Mary, who sat at the Lord's feet listening to what he said.' (Luke 10:38–39)

There were some homes that Jesus absolutely loved being in. One of them belonged to Martha and Mary, sisters who lived with their brother Lazarus in Bethany. I think that one meal they shared has been misunderstood. Preachers have often used this episode to contrast the life of quiet contemplation with one of bustling busyness. That's one element of the story, although there is no suggestion that contemplation is elevated above service. But the radical truth that emerges here is that Mary is placing herself in a position that was unheard of for women in Jesus' day: she is sitting at the feet of a rabbi.

Just as Saul of Tarsus sat 'at the feet of Gamaliel' (Acts 22:3, ESV), so now Mary behaves as if she were a man. In that culture, as in many parts of the world to this day, houses were divided into male 'space' and female 'space', and male and female roles were strictly demarcated as well. Mary had crossed an invisible but very important boundary within the house, and another equally important boundary within the social world.

Judaism did not forbid women to be instructed in the Torah but it was unheard of for a rabbi to allow a woman to sit at his feet. And far from rebuking her, commanding her to 'get back into her place', Jesus commends her. He truly is the liberator of women everywhere.

Some churches refuse to allow women to lead. Others even prohibit them from serving communion. And while the arguments are complex, these attitudes surely contradict Jesus' way.

He truly is the liberator of women

Prayer: Thank You, Lord Jesus, for the way You bring dignity and empowerment to all, regardless of gender. Amen.

Too busy

THURS 26 JAN

READ:
Luke 10:38–42
Psalm 37:1–7

FOCUS
'She came to him and asked, "Lord, don't you care that my sister has left me to do the work by myself? Tell her to help me!"'
(Luke 10:40)

Although, as we saw yesterday, this mealtime episode is not just about busyness, there's nodoubt that Jesus gently rebuked Martha for her well-intentioned but misplaced fussing. Whenwe're too busy, resentment builds within us. Martha might have been angry at Mary for being selfish (as she saw it) and she was also upset at Jesus because He was apparently encouraging Mary to sit and not to help. Perhaps she could be heard crashing pots around in the kitchen, occasionally putting her head into the room where Jesus and Mary were, and shooting her sister stern looks.

I've seen this in church life. Willing volunteers over-extend themselves by taking on too much, get exhausted, and then ultimately move to the edge or even drop out of their church because they are furious at the seeming passivity of others. They begin eagerly, and end irate.

An untamed diary leads to us not being fully present in the moment. Jesus was in the last six months of His ministry, and Martha was missing the opportunity to just be with Him. We've all seen people out for a meal together, but locked onto their phones. What a waste.

Finally, an untamed diary may lead us to give Jesus what He doesn't want. He wanted to be with Martha and Mary, rather than share in an elaborate meal. Keen Christians can be adept at doing things for God that He never asked for. Over-busy? It's time to change.

Prayer: Lord Jesus, show me today how to walk in a rhythm of life that pleases You and blesses me. Amen.

FRI 27 JAN

Multi-tasking

READ:
Luke 10:38–42
Matthew 6:25–34

FOCUS
'"Martha, Martha," the Lord answered, "you are worried and upset about many things, but few things are needed"' (Luke 10:41–42)

Picking up from where we were yesterday, it's worth saying that we are not only busier than ever, but we are endlessly multi-tasking. Thirty years ago, travel agents made our airline and rail reservations, salespeople assisted us in shops and professional typists helped busy people with their correspondence. Now in most cases we do many of those things ourselves.

We're an 'app' culture. We used to carry mobile phones, enabling us to make calls, and then texting was invented. Now that same device doubles as a platform for email, a calculator, web browser, appointment calendar, budget manager, music streamer, weather forecaster, GPS, tweeter, Facebook updater, and torch! And the list of available applications that we can use seems endless.

According to one survey, almost half of electronic tablet users over the age of 13 visit social networking sites, and 61% check their email while watching television. Even while relaxing, our brains are busier than ever before. We're assaulted with facts, pseudo-facts and rumour, all posing as information. Trying to figure out what you need to know and what you can ignore is exhausting.

Scientific research suggests that our brains are not wired to cope well with all this multi-tasking. We not only reduce focus and attention to detail when switching from one task to another, we also become less productive, and more prone to anxiety as our minds become increasingly over-cluttered.

So today, here's a thought: one thing at a time.

one thing at a time

Prayer: Grant me clarity to see what is really important today, and focus to accomplish what is really needed, Lord Jesus. Amen.

weekend

READ:

Ephesians 5:15–16 // Colossians 4:2–5

Simplify

Before we leave our conversations about the way we spend our time, it's important to pause and realise that we are called to take control. The Bible calls us to live carefully, to take responsibility. Jesus' gentle rebuke to Martha was a call to change. We're not told what her response was to what Jesus said. We can only hope she sat down and listened too!

Let's not live *under* our schedule, as if we're totally powerless to change anything, and let's be aware that we can hide behind our schedule. Busyness gives us a convenient excuse not to stop and think, or to avoid facing some uncomfortable truths about ourselves.

Perhaps we can respond by building 'technology breaks' into our schedule, both at work and at home. That might mean that we take some hours when we turn off our phones, silencing those distracting beeps. For a while, turn off your browser and email notifications as well. Have screen-free days!

We might avoid email and all screens for the first and last hour of the day so that our relationships, both with God and others, might get the attention they deserve.

To ponder: Are we willing to take small steps to simplify?

we are called to take control

What happened to Martha?

MON 30 JAN

READ:
John 11:17–27
John 12:1–3

FOCUS
'"Yes, Lord," she replied, "I believe that you are the Messiah, the Son of God, who is to come into the world."'
(John 11:27)

As we move on from this story, we could be tempted to think that Martha abandoned her propensity for serving and gave herself to a life of quiet contemplation. But there's no suggestion that this happened. Shattered by grief at the grave of her brother Lazarus, she expresses her faith in Jesus, telling Him that, if He had been there, death would not have taken her brother. There's no hint of criticism or reproach in her words, just a simple affirmation that she knew that Jesus had total authority, even over death – a remarkable declaration. And then, when the amazing meal was shared after Lazarus was raised, she is found serving once again.

Martha is also the one who thinks and speaks out one of the two great confessions about Christ in the New Testament. The other is Peter's in Matthew 16:16, but it was Martha who made the remarkable affirmation about Jesus being the Christ, the Son of God. Bear in mind that it was not at all in Jewish thinking that the Messiah would be God Himself, and so Martha's profession of faith is all the more amazing. She was not some bustling airhead, but someone who thought deeply and was receptive to the inspiration of the Holy Spirit.

Let's not succumb to the temptation to believe that there are some deeply spiritual souls who should only pray and contemplate, and in that find revelation, while others are 'just' practical, hardworking, but not very insightful. Martha was both. Let's know how to be still, and yet serve. Both matter.

Prayer: Father, let both stillness and serving be included in my day, this day. Amen.

TUES 31 JAN

Do as I do, or else

READ:
Luke 11:37–38
Galatians 1:11–13

FOCUS
'But the Pharisee was surprised when he noticed that Jesus did not first wash before the meal.' (Luke 11:38)

I've seen it too many times. Passionate Christians become convinced about an area of truth that becomes disproportionately important to them. They develop a view on the place of Israel in God's plan, or the importance of deliverance, methods of prayer with fasting, principles of faith and prosperity. They attend conferences, read books, converse with others who agree with their view. And then they decide that everyone else in their church needs to think this issue is as important as they do, and that if they don't, their commitment is lacking, their faith is deficient.

This is the second of three meals that Jesus shared with Pharisees described in Luke's Gospel. Jesus comes under direct criticism, this time because He did not follow the expected protocol for preparing for a meal. The hand-washing described here had nothing to do with hygiene, nor was it a ceremonial practice required by the Law. It was simply one of the endless rules followed by the Pharisees. It seems that some of the Pharisees were viewing Jesus as a legitimate 'rabbi' at this time, and so demanded that He follow the path that they followed. And that expectation ignited a very strong response from Jesus.

Be careful of misguided zeal that insists that everyone 'does faith' as you do. Paul was zealous as a Pharisee, but his zeal was terribly misguided. We all have different gifts, and a variety of opinions about what really is important. And we could be wrong.

Be careful of misguided zeal

Prayer: Father, grant me zeal with knowledge, and the humility to see that not everything is always as I see it. Amen.

Mealtime confrontation

WED 01 FEB

READ:
Luke 11:37–39
Hebrews 12:4–13

FOCUS
'Now then, you Pharisees clean the outside of the cup and dish, but inside you are full of greed and wickedness.' (Luke 11:39)

After speaking at a church in Texas, my family and I were lunching with the pastor, and were joined by another guest speaker who had a background in the IRA prior to his conversion. Suddenly the ex-IRA man made a very loud accusation across the table, and to my horror I realised that I was the accused. 'God has revealed to me that you hate the Irish. You're prejudiced against my people.' I was stunned. I spend a lot of time ministering in Ireland, in both the North and the Republic, and I love the land and the people. I stammered that he was wrong, hoping he would recognise his embarrassing mistake. But he was insistent. And his wife agreed.

During this meal with the Pharisee, Jesus revealed that He knew what was in the man's heart. Jesus was, of course, quite correct in His perception, and told the Pharisee so. Socially, it's rather unusual to enjoy hospitality and then inform your host that you believe that he (and his friends) are loaded with greed and wickedness. But then it is Jesus that we're talking about, the One who lovingly tells us the truth, rather than what we want to hear.

What happened during that meal in Texas? Unable to prove my accuser wrong, I politely excused myself and left the table. I just had to walk away. But if Jesus does some straight-talking, stay, listen, and heed His words. They might be difficult to hear, but are spoken for our good.

Prayer: Speak to me, Lord, even when what You have to say might be difficult to hear. Amen.

● THURS 02 FEB

Full of greed

READ:
Luke 11:37–39
Ephesians 5:1–3

FOCUS
'Now then, you Pharisees clean the outside of the cup and dish, but inside you are full of greed and wickedness.' (Luke 11:39)

Yesterday I wrote about being willing for God to challenge us. And today, I find myself personally under the spotlight of Holy Spirit-fuelled conviction, because I sense that the Lord has been warning me about greed. But this greedy attitude comes disguised, and works with subtlety. I tend to think of greed as being about always wanting more – an insatiable craving for more money, more food, more stuff. But as I've pondered this, I've realised that greed has many different faces, and can quietly wreak havoc in our lives.

As Jesus challenged the Pharisees about being 'full' of greed, He gave examples that exposed a general attitude of grabbing, rather than just outright gluttony or materialism.

In my case, I'm challenged about grasping onto, and therefore being greedy for, life. At 60, I'm increasingly aware that life has a horizon, and I don't like it. At times I feel like a child on a merry-go-round, loving the ride and wanting to cry at the thought of getting off. Holding on to life too tightly, I can squeeze the life out of life itself. Or I can be hungry for people to act the way I'd like them to act and, in trying to control them or being angry if they don't respond to me in the way I'd like, I'm greedy for them to act in the way that I want.

Let's ask the Lord to show us if there are subtle forms of greed nestling in us, and live with more open hearts and hands today.

live with more open hearts and hands

Prayer: When greed disguises itself, reveal it, Lord, and help me to overcome it. Amen.

What to give away

FRI 03 FEB

READ:
Luke 11:39–41
Hebrews 12:1–3

FOCUS
'But now as for what is inside you – be generous to the poor, and everything will be clean for you.' (Luke 11:41)

I mentioned earlier that we tend to think of the Pharisees in purely negative terms, the 'bad guys' of the Gospels. It's not surprising that we jump to that conclusion, because some of them did dog Jesus' footsteps at every turn (that's especially evident in Matthew's Gospel) and Jesus reserved His most scathing words of rebuke for them. But if we're not careful, we can think that we are surely much better than the Pharisees. Actually, many of their sins are ours, and in some respects, they showed greater dedication than a lot of us Christians. One example is in their giving. Although their fussy attitude towards tithing blinded them to the need to care for the poor, the fact is that they did give. Most church leaders will agree that the financial challenges that churches usually face would be resolved overnight if the majority of church members gave appropriately, but they do not.

So let's not write the Pharisees off as men who were not wholly committed to religion as they viewed it. Sadly, their commitment was selective. They gave, but then gossiped and plotted Jesus' downfall. They were fastidious about their rules and regulations, but proud with it, as we'll see tomorrow. And so Jesus told them to 'give away' their greed (the words about giving to the poor are not in the original Greek). In other words, Jesus was calling for an offering where we 'donate' our bad attitudes. Is there an attitude or sin that, figuratively speaking, needs to go in the offering basket?

Prayer: Help me to 'give', to throw off sins and habits that trip me up, loving Father. Amen.

weekend

READ:
Luke 11:42–54 //
Ephesians 4:29–32

Other symptoms of greed

Yesterday we saw that greed can manifest itself in our lives in many different ways. In confronting the Pharisees, Jesus exposed their grabbing hearts.

They were meticulous tithers, but felt that their religious giving exempted them from the need to care for the poor and marginalised – an attitude that God quite literally hates.

Gluttonous for power, they insisted that the coveted 'best' seats in the synagogues were theirs and theirs alone. Hungry for applause, they swept through the market-places, gathering respectful nods and muttered plaudits.

And there was tragic irony about them, because the Pharisees spent their lives worrying about being ritually clean (and cajoled others to do the same). Jesus exposed them as being full of corruption and filth. Stepping on a grave rendered a person unclean, and so the graves were whitewashed, to clearly identify them. But the Pharisees were like 'unmarked' graves. People who came into contact with them may have been fooled into believing that they were encountering holy men, but in fact they were soiled by the experience.

To ponder: When people meet us, are they blessed or brought down?

there was tragic irony about them

CWR

Helping others live life God's way

CWR's ministry extends around the globe. Our resources are shipped to Australia and New Zealand, with thousands of free Bible reading notes also being sent into Australian prisons each month.

Our partner in Nigeria prints and distributes around 100,000 daily devotionals six times a year and we have national distributors in over 14 different countries. We train counsellors in Singapore, provide resources in Malaysia, and are beginning to offer teaching in Cambodia.

God has opened doors for us to have several of our publications and teaching materials translated into Mandarin, Farsi, Tamil, Sinhala, Korean, Finnish and Welsh – to name but a few! These incredible opportunities are only possible with God's grace and your valued prayers and donations that come from all over the world.

Every day, God continues to provide opportunities to cross borders and reach more people with His life-changing Word. Thank you for your continued support for the international work that we are doing.

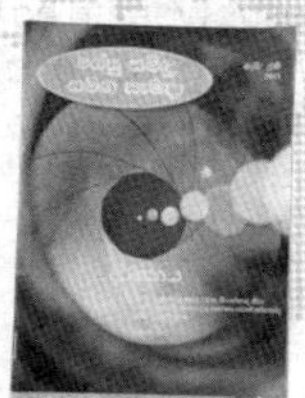

If you would like to make a donation to our work around the world, please fill in the 'Gift to CWR' section on the order form at the back of these Bible reading notes, completing the Gift Aid declaration if appropriate.

● MON 06 FEB

Looking for trouble

READ:
Luke 14:1–14
Jude 16

FOCUS
'One Sabbath, when Jesus went to eat in the house of a prominent Pharisee, he was being carefully watched.' (Luke 14:1)

It was the perfect set-up. In working a plan to trap Jesus, the Pharisees had created a foolproof strategy to ensnare Him, or so they thought. But before we consider their scheme in more detail, it's worth noticing the posture of Jesus' critics. They were carefully watching Him, eager to find fault, ready to discover opportunities for offence. I've met Christians like that, and sometimes, I'm sad to say, I've been one of those Christians. They go to church on the hunt for trouble. Perhaps the worship group that week is not to their liking. Before anyone plays a note, the wannabe-offended are ready, waiting for an off-key note, a missed beat, for the volume to be too loud, or the song selection not to be to their liking. And the sad truth is that prejudice is blind, noticing only the faults that confirm our suspicions, while often impervious to the good things in others. Prejudice looks for confirmation, and edits out contradiction.

Is there someone in your life, church or workplace that you are 'carefully watching', not because they are worthy of suspicion, but because you're keen to catch them in the wrong? It's an exhausting, soul-destroying pastime. Don't be a fault-finder. Those who look for faults will usually find something to be irritated about, if they wait long enough. Why not abandon the surveillance routine, and instead, see if you can catch that person doing something right? Or ask yourself why you're doing this, and see if you can resolve it.

Don't be a fault-finder

Prayer: Lord, I don't want to give myself to fault-finding. Rescue me from the blindness of prejudice, today and always. Amen.

What don't we see about us?

TUES 07 FEB

READ:
Luke 14:1–4
Matthew 7:3–5

FOCUS
'Jesus asked the Pharisees and experts in the law, "Is it lawful to heal on the Sabbath or not?" But they remained silent.' (Luke 14:3–4)

As a speaker and writer, I am constantly outlining principles, exhorting people to embrace kingdom attitudes. But there is danger in what I do. Dealing with so many words, spoken and written, can cause me to become insensitive to the need for *me* to live according to those biblical principles.

In the first of four mealtime conversations in this single episode, Jesus responds to the Pharisees' question with a question – a popular Jewish teaching habit. Someone asked a rabbi, 'Why do you always answer questions with questions?' He replied, 'What's wrong with questions?' As we saw yesterday, the Pharisees were trying to trap Jesus by setting Him up with a Sabbath day opportunity that could establish Him as a Sabbath-breaker. A very sick man was at the meal, and they knew that Jesus not only had power, but also a tender heart. Surely He would heal him, and His guilt would be proven. But Jesus brilliantly turned the tables on them, responding with a double question that would convict *them* either as Sabbath-breakers, or as heartless souls who didn't care about people. The Pharisees were keen to call Jesus to account, but remained stubbornly silent when they were quizzed.

Sometimes we see faults in others with great clarity, while either being oblivious to or deliberately ignoring our own sins. Pray today's prayer regularly, and respond when God answers.

Prayer: Holy Spirit, please show me what I don't see about myself. Amen.

WED 08 FEB

A greater law

READ:
Luke 14:1–6
Luke 13:15–17

FOCUS
'Then he asked them, "If one of you has a child or an ox that falls into a well on the Sabbath day, will you not immediately pull it out?"' (Luke 14:5)

Eric Liddell, the Olympic gold medal-winning athlete whose story was told in the film *Chariots of Fire*, was celebrated for his faithful refusal to compete on the Sabbath. While not everyone would agree with his interpretation of the Sabbath day principle, none could question his commitment to what he believed was right. Having gone to China as a missionary, Liddell died as a relatively young man, just over twenty years later in a Japanese internment camp.

There was some freedom of activity allowed within the camp, and Liddell was responsible for overseeing sporting activities. One of the hardest decisions he had to make in the camp was what to do about Sunday games. He prohibited them because of his principles. But many of the teenagers protested about this and decided to organise a game by themselves, boys against girls. It ended in a big fight, because there was no referee. Liddell would not run on a Sunday for an Olympic gold medal and all the glory in the world; but he decided to referee games on Sundays, just to keep a handful of imprisoned youngsters at peace with each other. He realised compassion was more important than cherished principles.

Working to rescue a stranded ox was clearly forbidden by the Pharisees, but they would surely allow it out of concern for the animal. Jesus argued that if they cared for their animals in that way, surely concern for humans was more important than Sabbath day principles?

Compassion was more important

Prayer: May I never become so committed to principle that I become oblivious to the needs of people, loving God. Amen.

Humility and pride

● THURS 09 FEB

READ:
Luke 14:7–11
1 John 2:15–17

FOCUS
'For all those who exalt themselves will be humbled, and those who humble themselves will be exalted.' (Luke 14:11)

Success in any field can be highly dangerous, and can ruin us. When we're blessed, having achieved something noteworthy in the eyes of others, we face the temptation of pride. People say overly nice things about us. Accolades pile up. And before long, we start to believe that we are special, above the rest of the run-of-the-mill souls. We've gained applause, and lost our humility.

This happens in churches. Years ago, I was part of a great church that was filled with passionately committed people. It was an honour to be part of what God was doing among us. Congregations were being planted, and such was the level of zeal, some people sold their homes (losing money in days of negative equity) so that they could relocate to serve as part of that planting strategy. I look back on that season in my life with great affection and gratitude.

But I wonder sometimes whether we started to think that we were more radical, more in tune with what God was doing, more contemporary than any other church. Held in high esteem by Christian leaders and congregations around the nation, I think that a little pride crept in, at least into my own heart, and I can only speak for myself.

Pride is subtle. And ironically, it can shame us. Portraying the awkward embarrassment of a dinner guest who has picked a place of high honour at a meal only to be told to move when a more 'important' guest shows up, Jesus teaches us not to be haughty, either with each other or, surely, in the presence of God.

Prayer: I would rather humble myself than have You be forced to humble me, Lord. Show me how to live in authentic humility. Amen.

FRI 10 FEB

Inviting the unlikely

READ:
Luke 14:12–24
James 1:26–27

FOCUS
'But when you give a banquet, invite the poor, the crippled, the lame, the blind, and you will be blessed.' (Luke 14:13–14)

In His third comment at the table, Jesus speaks broadly about unexpected guests who will be invited to the kingdom banquet. Remember Jesus came to Israel first, and many Jews became followers of Christ, but the nation as a whole largely rejected Him. It had always been the intention to throw open the doors of welcome to the Gentiles. This idea, while repeated in Scripture, was still shocking to the Jews at the time, and it took the Church a long time to accept that Gentiles could be saved without observing all the Jewish laws.

But in looking at the broad interpretation of the parable in the second part of the reading, we mustn't ignore the first part, which is a rather strange command to invite unlikely strangers for meals rather than close friends. This was accomplished more easily in the ancient world, when homes were much more open and people would wander into a home during meals unchallenged – we see this happening in the Gospel accounts frequently. But even though culture and practice are different now, and meals are shared behind closed doors, let's not miss the challenge to reach out to those who are often overlooked. And that doesn't involve just sharing the message in words, but embodying the message in service, hospitality, and care. When churches serve their communities (as they do in countless ways across the UK), volunteer in food banks or welcome refugees, they are not just do-gooders, they reflect the heartbeat of the kingdom, and of the King.

Prayer: How easy it is to become preoccupied with my own life, Lord. Help me to see those who are often overlooked. Amen.

READ:
Luke 19:1–10 //
Acts 9:1-6

The man in the tree

Danny DeVito in a tree: that's how I picture Zacchaeus. He was not only one of the hated tax collectors, but was a chief tax collector. He probably had his own network of tax officials, creaming money from their profits, as well as practising his own extortionate trade. His wealth would have been immense. Taxes were collected at three places inland (Capernaum, Jericho, and Jerusalem) and he had one of the big three territories. But when we first meet him, before he shared a meal with Jesus, we find him perched up a tree – a rather comical figure. God was stirring something in his heart, which began with curiosity. He wanted to see Jesus.

Today I met with a man in a professional capacity, in a situation where it would have been inappropriate for me to talk about faith. A sworn atheist, he said, 'Once our work is done today, can we talk about God, please? I believe that our meeting together was meant to be.'

God is able to stir the hearts of those who seem unreachable, like Zacchaeus, like Saul. Take hope today in that truth. I will.

To ponder: Who in your life seems unreachable for Christ? Pray that God will impact them with His love.

our meeting together was meant to be

Discover the Holy Land

WITH JEFF AND KAY LUCAS

Join us to explore and enjoy many of the amazing sights of Jerusalem and the simple beauty of Galilee. Choose from one of these upcoming trips:
Mon–Mon, 27 March – 3 April 2017
Tues–Tues, 2–9 May 2017

We'll visit some key biblical locations, starting in **Upper Galilee** and the **Jordan Valley**. We'll drive through the **Hula Valley** and along the **Eastern Shore of Galilee**, with a stop at **Bethsaida**, before passing **Jericho** and ascending to **Jerusalem**. No visit to Jerusalem would be complete without a stop at the **Western (Wailing) Wall** and the **Temple Mount**, **St Stephen's Gate**, the **Pool of Bethesda** and the **Via Dolorosa**.

Other highlights will be a visit to the **Mount of Olives**, the **Garden of Gethsemane** and the **Garden Tomb**, where there will be an opportunity for shared Communion. Also, we'll visit

Bethlehem and view the **Church of the Nativity** and the **Shepherds' Fields**, and have an opportunity to hear about local community work there. We'll travel down the **Jericho Road** to the lowest point on earth at approximately 1,300 feet below sea level, enjoy a visit to **Qumran**, where the Dead Sea Scrolls were found, and then ascend to the **summit of Masada** by cable car to hear its amazing story.

Last, we visit the **Israel Museum** to see the Dead Sea Scrolls and the stunning Holyland Model of Jerusalem, showing the city as it may well have been in the time of Jesus, before a final visit to the **Old City** for some haggling or simple relaxation. Kay and I would be delighted to have you with us.

For booking details call Josh on **07947604812** or email **tours@travelinkuk.com** or **groups@travelinkuk.com**

● MON 13 FEB

Unexpected grace

READ:
Luke 19:1–6
1 Corinthians 1:26–31

FOCUS
'So he came down at once and welcomed him gladly.'
(Luke 19:6)

In his brilliant book *Messy Spirituality*, the late Mike Yaconelli confessed that he used to dream a recurring dream where he would be in a crowd around Jesus, who would point in his direction and say, 'Follow me.' Mike's heart would leap, and he would begin running towards Jesus, only to hear Him say, 'No, I'm sorry, I wasn't calling you. I was talking to the person behind you.' Many of us can understand that feeling, that fear. We humans can have an unusual trait when it comes to God. We tend to count ourselves out when there is talk of God's blessing, grace, and approval, thinking that really good news must be for somebody else, not us. And we count ourselves in when there is talk of divine judgment and anger.

When Jesus drew near to the sycamore tree that Zacchaeus was perched in, I imagine that the little tax-gatherer tensed. He had been the rotten man, responsible for misery in so many lives because of his organised extortion. Perhaps he broke into a sweat. But even then, did Zacchaeus think that it was surely reckoning time now? In a sense it would be: everything would change, but that change would come as a result of joy, and a shared meal. He would voluntarily make restitution, but not because he felt condemned. Whatever the table talk that occurred between Jesus and Zacchaeus, the warmth of it birthed a hunger for a personal revolution.

Jesus looked up and called Zacchaeus. And He has called us. Yes, that would be you, and me too.

Prayer: Thank You for calling me to Yourself, Lord, for welcoming me into Your family. Amen.

He has called us

Loosening our grip

● TUES 14 FEB

READ:
Luke 19:1–8
Deuteronomy 15:1–11

FOCUS
'But Zacchaeus stood up and said ... "Look, Lord! Here and now I give half of my possessions to the poor, and if I have cheated ... I will pay back four times the amount."'
(Luke 19:8)

Get a grip. It's a saying that encourages us to take control, seize the opportunity, take the helm in our lives and emotions. But as I mentioned earlier, I've been sensing God's call to loosen my grip on life, and that call and challenge has some very practical consequences. We can hold too tightly to things, to money, to our goals, and to our time.

In Zacchaeus' case, it was cash that he gripped. He had not only worked hard to build his seedy but highly profitable empire, but he would have sacrificed greatly to get to where he was, losing his social status, becoming one of the despised Roman lackeys because of his profession. He loved money that much. Now his grip on 'stuff' relaxes, and he begins to live open-handedly, all because of Jesus. The grabber becomes an extravagant giver, paying back way beyond what was required of him.

Kent Hughes, commenting on this beautiful episode, says, 'The demands of the gospel are intensely practical, and they include a reorientation to one's material possessions. One's grip on things is dramatically loosened.'* When we loosen our grip, we are more ready to share, to give, to make space, to make allowances. We see ourselves as stewards of what we have, rather than owners. And instead of being people who offer minimums, we become generous people – even, at times, extravagant, if our resources allow it. Today, with your time, talent and treasure, don't get a grip. The world will be better for it. And ironically, you'll be happier.

Prayer: Open-handed, open-hearted; help me to live with those attitudes today, for Your glory, Father. Amen.

*R. Kent Hughes, *Luke: that you may know the truth* (Wheaton, Illinois: Crossway Books, 1988) p225

WED 15 FEB

Here and now

READ:
Luke 19:8–10
Hebrews 3:12–15

FOCUS
'Zacchaeus ... said ... "Look, Lord! ... I give half of my possessions to the poor, and if I have cheated anybody out of anything, I will pay back four times the amount."' (Luke 19:8)

I've seen it too often, both in others, and sadly, in myself. We are stirred in church and feel compelled to promise God something. Our pledge is sincere. But then the music fades, and with it, our vow. The kingdom revolution has come to the little tax collector in the person of Jesus. And so he immediately decides – from this moment, 'here and now' – everything is going to be very different. He doesn't close down his business and join the band of men who had left their jobs to follow Jesus as His disciples. Instead, he determines that, in staying in his world, he will do business with absolute integrity from now on. But what is startling is the decisiveness that he demonstrates. As Zacchaeus makes a very precise promise about disposing of half of his net worth in gifts to the poor, and restoring funds to people that he had cheated at a whopping 400% interest rate, he stands to his feet to make the announcement, rather than just whispering his decision to Jesus.

This was not the proud show of piety that the Pharisees were guilty of when they gave, desperate to draw attention to themselves. Instead, Zacchaeus was surely making his decision public so that he would be held accountable for following through. It would also serve as an announcement so that word would get out, and those cheated could come and make their claim! When God speaks, let's act. Immediately.

Prayer: Speak Lord, and when You do, help me to respond with action. Amen.

Jesus in control

THURS 16 FEB

READ:
Luke 22:1–13
Romans 12:1–2

FOCUS
'He will show you a large room upstairs, all furnished. Make preparations there.' (Luke 22:12)

The heat was on. By now, the religious barons were desperate to get rid of Jesus. And behind their urgent scheming we see the hand of Satan too, as Judas' identity as the betrayer is confirmed. Satan has filled his heart. But Jesus wants to celebrate this meal with His friends, not only because this will be the last Passover they share before His death, but because, as we'll see, it was so loaded with significance. The memory of it would help them through the difficult days to come. Careful, secret arrangements had to be made for the celebration. If Judas knew the location, then the arrest would happen, thwarting the plans for the meal. And so the trusted pair from Jesus' inner circle, Peter and John, are tasked with the job of completing the arrangement in locating a private room and buying the lamb for the meal. At the same time, an elaborate hush-hush meeting has been organised by Jesus, involving an unknown man who would be identifiable because he would be carrying a water jar, an action usually only carried out by women – men carried water skins.

Jesus made special and meticulous arrangements. He is not dragged towards His death, but resolutely marches in that direction. He was not killed as the victim of cruel circumstances, but rather, He laid down His life voluntarily for us. Let's give thanks today for His intentional love for us. And let's follow His example, and intentionally offer ourselves as living sacrifices today.

Prayer: Willingly, intentionally, I offer myself for Your purposes, Father. Amen.

FRI 17 FEB

A Passover meal

READ:
Luke 22:1–23
John 1:29

FOCUS
'And he said to them, "I have eagerly desired to eat this Passover with you before I suffer."' (Luke 22:15)

Two thousand years ago, Jerusalem would have been teeming with pilgrims. Some ancient historians claimed that three million descended upon the ancient city, but these figures were almost certainly exaggerated. Modern scholars put the number at 200,000, which would still have made for a packed little city. The narrow alleys were jammed with beggars, and traders selling the major purchase of the festival: the Passover lambs or goats. The mass slaughtering of the animals was accomplished in three shifts. And then, in the evening, people would join together for the Passover meal, which includes bitter herbs to remind everyone of the bitter days of slavery in Egypt, and the roasted lamb, which brought to mind the blood of the lamb placed on the doorposts of every Jewish house.

Jesus chose this event to be the backdrop for His cosmos-shaking work on the cross. The symbolism is obvious. Just as Moses had led his people out of slavery at the Passover, so Jesus, in His exodus or departure (Luke 9) would lead all who trust Him out of the captivity of sin and death. He would be the Lamb of God who would mysteriously accomplish that freedom, shedding His own blood to save us. Judgment passes over us, just as the angel of death passed over the homes where blood was applied. It is not because of our good works, but because of His great work, giving His very life for us. The Lamb of God has taken away our sins. We remember, thankfully: grace is free, but it isn't cheap.

Prayer: You paid the price that You did not owe, Lamb of God, for me. I praise You. Thank You. Amen.

READ:
Luke 22:1–23 //
Exodus 31:1–5

Weekend

Creative communication

I love to see the Church being creative. When we celebrate the work and insights of the poets, dancers, actors, painters, sculptors, not only do they find joy in expressing their worship in a way that is meaningful to them, but the Church is enriched by the fresh dimensions that their creativity brings. But even more than that, their artistry points to the Creator God.

I have been frequently asked, 'Where do you find all this creativity in the Bible?' My response has been, 'Right from the very start – in the beginning, God created!' Throughout Scripture, through the priests in their colourful robes, the smell of the incense, the architecture of the tent and Temple, the call to God's people to celebrate the feasts and festivals that dramatically retold the story of God, we see the consistent golden thread of creativity. And here, as Jesus edges closer to the cross and tries to prepare His disciples for the harrowing time ahead, He gave them a meal as a message, rather than words. Celebrate the creatives in your church: they have a vital part in communicating the big story.

To ponder: Preaching tends to be elevated above other forms of communication. Why? Should it be that way?

● MON 20 FEB

Truth revealed

READ:
Luke 22:24–38
James 1:22–25

FOCUS
'A dispute also arose among them as to which of them was considered to be greatest.' (Luke 22:24)

I touched on this earlier, but it's worth repeating. Recently I've been praying: 'Lord, show me what it is about me that I don't see.' We all have blind spots, especially when it comes to our own faults and weaknesses. We may have 20/20 vision when it comes to seeing the wrong in others, yet be oblivious to what is going on in us. That's one reason why we all need trusted friends whom we've given permission to tell the truth as they see it to us. At the supper, so much is revealed. The traditional Passover cups are invested with new meaning, pointing to the truths of the new covenant that Jesus has made now with us. Assurance of eternity is given, as Jesus speaks of a day when He will drink a glass of wine with His people in the great kingdom banquet to come.

But the truth is revealed about people as well. The disciples are shown in an ugly portrait of competitiveness, arguing about who is the greatest. The identity of the betrayer becomes known, as Judas slips away into the darkness to do his terrible work. And Peter, so headstrong and confident, convinced that he will be faithful to Jesus, is told that within hours he will crumble. He seems quite oblivious to the possibility, but Jesus makes it clear: denial will come, not just once, but three times.

Perhaps God is trying to get our attention about a glaring flaw in us. It may be that God's method of speaking to us is through a friend who is trying to point out some unwelcome truths to us. Let's listen.

God is trying to get our attention

Prayer: Lord, by Your Spirit, by whatever means or method You choose, show me what I do not see about myself. Amen.

On the road

TUES 21 FEB

READ:
Luke 24:13–16
John 20:11–18

FOCUS
'Jesus himself came up and walked along with them; but they were kept from recognising him.' (Luke 24:15–16)

It's a famous moment in the vintage *Bugs Bunny* cartoon series. The diminutive Elmer Fudd, ever grumpy and keen to track the cheeky rabbit down, is holding his gun – the attentive hunter – when Bugs approaches him, stands right next to him, and asks the question he always asks: 'What's up, doc?'

'Be very, very quiet,' whispers Elmer. 'I'm hunting wabbits.' The absurdity of the moment is obvious. Elmer wants to focus on looking for Bugs, while Bugs is actually standing right next to him, having a chat.

On the Emmaus road, Jesus strolls alongside a couple (probably Cleopas, the brother of Joseph, Jesus' father; the other person may have been Cleopas' wife). They are talking about Jesus to Jesus, but are unaware that it is Him. The statement 'they were kept from recognising Him' has often been interpreted to mean that somehow God prevented them from seeing who Christ was, but the scripture isn't emphatic about that – the word used just means 'their eyes were under arrest'. It may well have been tiredness and the fact that they just didn't expect to see Him, believing Him to be dead, that prevented them from realising that Jesus was right there. And later they *would* understand, once He had blessed the bread.

I'd like Jesus to make His presence a little more obvious in my life. But I wonder how often He has been quietly at work without me realising, speaking to me without me hearing, walking with me without me acknowledging His presence. How about you?

Prayer: Thank You for walking with me and working in me, Jesus, even when I don't notice. Amen.

● WED 22 FEB

Going the wrong way

READ:
Luke 24:13–27
Acts 26:12–18

FOCUS
'Jesus himself came up and walked along with them.' (Luke 24:15)

It's a heart-wrenching challenge that many of us have to live with. Having raised our children to love God, some of them have marched or drifted away, apparently indifferent now to all that they knew and experienced in their younger years. In some cases, not only are they angry with God, but they're upset with us too. Some *Life Every Day* readers will be in a situation where they don't even know where their adult children are, or if they're safe. A ringing phone in the middle of the night brings instant terror. And obviously it's not just parents who experience the pain of loving someone who, apparently at least, no longer loves God (I say apparently, because sometimes people walk away from faith not because they want to abandon God, but because they are trying to find Him for real). Some grieve for husbands, mothers, and friends.

The good news is that Jesus is able to meet with them. It might not happen because they come back to church and have an encounter, and it may have nothing to do with us. God is out there on the road. We can pray that they will have an undeniable experience of the love of God.

The Emmaus pair were heading in the wrong direction – and it wouldn't be long before they would make a 180-degree turn and make the dangerous late evening trek seven miles back to the city of Jerusalem. But before a meal was shared, Jesus walked with them even as they were heading the wrong way. And He can do that for those we love who are heading the wrong way too.

Jesus is able to meet with them

Prayer: I am so grateful, Lord, that You can meet those I love on the road, even when they are walking in the wrong direction. Amen.

NEXT ISSUE

Pressure Points

MAR/APR 2017

Life brings pressure – whether it's the pressure of making good decisions, steering through sickness or handling conflict. We read in Matthew that 'Each day has enough trouble of its own', and Christians aren't promised a life without pressure. Actually, we can experience additional stresses because of our desire to live a life that is pleasing to God, including the pressures of living right, working for kingdom justice, and simply continuing to believe in and trust God.

In the next issue of *Life Every Day* we will take a look at some of our everyday pressures, and prayerfully consider our responses to these pressures that we all experience.

Obtain your copy from CWR or a Christian bookshop

Also available as eBook/eSubscription

THURS 23 FEB

Disappointment

READ:
Luke 24:13–24
Jonah 4:1–11

FOCUS
'He asked them, "What are you discussing together as you walk along?" They stood still, their faces downcast.' (Luke 24:17)

Disappointment: it comes to us all. Anyone who has hopes or expectations in life eventually comes to the place where they realise that all is not going to turn out as they anticipated. The marriage is no longer as vibrant, the children seem distant and ungrateful, the new church that looked so promising seems flat and irrelevant. Sickness comes and healing doesn't follow. Prayers are prayed fervently, and yet heaven seems like brass. Disappointment with God is a feeling not only shared by many Christians, but the Bible describes the experiences of many of the 'greats' in God's story (like David, Elijah, and Jonah) who came to the place of feeling disenchanted with the Lord because all had not turned out as they hoped.

Before the beautiful meal when Jesus' identity was revealed to the Emmaus pair, they shared their disappointment with the unknown stranger who was strolling with them. The picture Luke paints is one of utter despair as they stop on the road, immobilised by their own sadness. And their statement is one that we can use as a prayer: 'we had hoped' (v21).

But their hopes were built on misunderstanding. The common view among the Jews was that a Messiah figure would come, overthrow the hated puppet king, Herod, and his Roman overlords, and establish Israel as a monarchy. But this was never Jesus' intention, and He never promised that He would do any such thing. Feel free to pray 'we had hoped', but make sure that you're not disappointed unreasonably.

Prayer: Lord, thank You I can pray 'I had hoped', but may I not be disappointed when You don't deliver what You didn't promise. Amen.

The playful Jesus

FRI 24 FEB

READ:
Luke 24:25–32
Matthew 19:13–14

FOCUS
'As they approached the village to which they were going, Jesus continued on as if he were going further.' (Luke 24:28)

Jesus was having fun, and playing a joke, twice in one encounter. It might be an idea that some are uncomfortable with. I'm occasionally asked if I think that Jesus ever laughed; a strange question. He was a popular party guest, and not just because of His wisdom or power (or because He was rather good with water and wine!). Small children seemed at ease with Him – they are not usually at home with intense, serious strangers. And here, as a prelude to a shared meal, Jesus seems to be enjoying a playful moment. First of all, as the disappointed pair talk about the tumultuous events of the last few days in Jerusalem, He asks, 'What things?' He obviously knew, seeing as He had been at the very centre of the arrest, trial, execution and resurrection, but He pretends not to know to allow them to share their perspective. And if we're uncomfortable with the thought of Jesus pretending, look at what He did when they arrived in Emmaus – we read that Jesus 'acted as if He were going further'. The word translated 'acted' is *prospoio*, which means 'pretended'. Of course, His playful touch here was constructive – this was not at the expense of Cleopas and his travelling companion, and ultimately enabled some life-changing instruction. But it's still a delightful and perhaps unexpected sight.

If your concept of Jesus is of an unendingly stern, forever intense Victorian man who rarely smiles and is disgusted by even good, clean fun, then your picture of Him is wrong.

Prayer: Help me to discover more of Your delightful personality, Lord Jesus. Amen.

Jesus was having fun

Weekend

25/26 FEB

READ:

Luke 24:28–32 //
Revelation 3:20

Inviting Jesus in for supper

Over the last couple of months, as we've been looking at the meals that Jesus shared (as recorded by Luke), we've seen that there were times when He literally invited Himself over for lunch; an action that was unusual socially (both then and now), but one that brought revolution, notably in the life of a racketeer tax collector called Zacchaeus.

But generally, guests wait for an invitation, and Jesus is no exception. It seems that His little ruse was intentional, because the Emmaus pair strongly reacts to it: 'But they urged him strongly, "Stay with us, for it is nearly evening; the day is almost over." So he went in to stay with them' (v29). The word that is used here is more intense than a polite but pressing invitation – it carries the idea of force. These two were insistent, even adamant. They wanted this unknown traveller to share supper with them.

Jesus goes where He's wanted – He doesn't barge into our lives. And I think it's healthy to ensure that we keep inviting Him in for each phase and season. Have you remembered to do this? What about now?

To ponder: How are you different from the person that you were a decade ago? Is it time to affirm your commitment to Christ now?

He doesn't barge into our lives

Right away

● MON 27 FEB

READ:
Luke 24:33–35
Hebrews 4:7

FOCUS
'They got up and returned at once to Jerusalem.' (Luke 24:33)

As we begin to draw our study of the meals of Jesus to a close, I've been struck once again by how being around Jesus prompted immediate, decisive action. Those who shared table talk with Him didn't just go away, ponder what they'd heard, and then make incremental, gradual shifts in their lives. They made sudden decisions that took effect immediately; decisions that must have stunned those around them. Remember Zacchaeus and his 'here and now' speech? There was a man who threw himself headlong into a brand-new way of living. And here, having had their hearts 'strangely warmed' by being around Jesus, hearing His exposition of Scripture and then sharing supper with Him, the Emmaus two jump up and head back for Jerusalem. They could have been forgiven for resting overnight and then heading back in the warmth and safety of a new day – but their response was instant. Luke wants us to see – this trip was taken 'at once'.

While I don't want to encourage rash, impetuous decisions that are not thought through (Scripture tells us to be people who carefully count the cost of commitment, and that our giving, for example, should come from careful reflection), I don't want to procrastinate either. At the end of the road back to Jerusalem, a joyful party awaited. When God clearly shows us what steps we should take, let's step out, assured of His presence and help, however shadowy and perilous the road might appear to be.

Prayer: Help me to see, to hear, and to act decisively, Lord. Amen.

● TUES 28 FEB

READ:
Luke 24:36–53
Revelation 19:1–10

FOCUS
'They gave him a piece of broiled fish, and he took it and ate it in their presence.'
(Luke 24:42–43)

Fit for earth and heaven

We end our time with a brief look at the last meal that Luke records Jesus sharing in his Gospel (Jesus also shared meals with the disciples in the six post-resurrection/pre-ascension weeks that are recorded in Acts). Here we see a group of disciples who, true to form, are mystified – 'startled and frightened' as Luke puts it – bewildered by Jesus' appearing to them, thinking He is a ghost, and needing clarity about what kind of body He has. Jesus attempts to show them the physicality of His body by inviting them to see His wounds and touch His skin, and then eating a piece of broiled fish to emphasise the point. He really does have a body of flesh, but one that is like no other, because He can appear at will, yet still eat. This is a resurrection body.

People often ask me what I think heaven will be like, and there are a few books that have become best-sellers, describing people's post-death experiences with detail that may or may not be helpful. What we do know is that heaven will not be about ethereally floating around on clouds. We will have resurrection bodies that are solid but are unlike what we have now, because they will be fit for earth as well as heaven. Ultimately, the new Jerusalem is coming down to earth, and we will share in yet another meal with Jesus – this time, one that heralds the fullness of eternity being ours – the marriage supper of the Lamb. What a feast, what a celebration that will be.

what a celebration that will be

Prayer: God, I thank You for the sure and certain hope of the resurrection to come. In the meantime, help me to walk with You. Amen.

Order form

LED J/F 2017

5 Easy Ways To Order

1. Phone in your credit card order: **01252 784700** (Mon–Fri, 9.30am – 5pm)
2. Visit our online store at **www.cwr.org.uk/store**
3. Send this form together with your payment to: **CWR, Waverley Abbey House, Waverley Lane, Farnham, Surrey GU9 8EP**
4. Visit a Christian bookshop
5. For Australia and New Zealand visit KI Entertainment **www.cwr4u.net.au**

For a list of our National Distributors, who supply countries outside the UK, visit **www.cwr.org.uk/distributors**

Your Details (required for orders and donations)

Full Name:	**CWR ID No.** (if known):
Home Address:	
	Postcode:
Telephone No. (for queries):	**Email:**

Publications

TITLE	QTY	PRICE	TOTAL
Total Publications			
UK P&P: up to £24.99 = **£2.99**; £25.00 and over = **FREE**			
Elsewhere P&P: up to £10 = **£4.95**; £10.01 – £50 = **£6.95**; £50.01 – £99.99 = **£10**; £100 and over = **£30**			
Total Publications and P&P (please allow 14 days for delivery)		**A**	

All CWR adult Bible reading notes are also available in **eBook** and **email subscription** format. Visit **www.cwr.org.uk** for further information.

Subscriptions* (non direct debit)

Subscriptions* (non direct debit)	QTY	PRICE (including P&P) UK	Europe	Elsewhere	TOTAL
Every Day with Jesus (1yr, 6 issues)		£15.95	£19.95	Please contact nearest National Distributor or CWR direct	
Large Print *Every Day with Jesus* (1yr, 6 issues)		£15.95	£19.95		
Inspiring Women Every Day (1yr, 6 issues)		£15.95	£19.95		
Life Every Day (Jeff Lucas) (1yr, 6 issues)		£15.95	£19.95		
Mettle: 15–18s (1yr, 3 issues)		£14.50	£16.60		
YP's: 11–14s (1yr, 6 issues)		£15.95	£19.95		
Topz: 7–11s (1yr, 6 issues)		£15.95	£19.95		
Cover to Cover Every Day	Email subscription only, to order visit online store.				
Total Subscriptions (subscription prices already include postage and packing)				**B**	

Please circle which issue you would like your subscription to commence from:

JAN/FEB MAR/APR MAY/JUN JUL/AUG SEP/OCT NOV/DEC *Mettle* **JAN–APR MAY–AUG SEP–DEC**

*Only use this section for subscriptions paid for by credit/debit card or cheque. For Direct Debit subscriptions see overleaf.

We promise to never share your details with other charities. By giving us your personal information, you agree that we may use this to send you information about the ministry of CWR. If you do not want to receive further information by post, please tick here. ☐

Continued overleaf >>

<< See previous page for start of order form

Payment Details

☐ I enclose a cheque/PO made payable to CWR for the amount of: £ ____________

☐ Please charge my credit/debit card.

Cardholder's Name (in BLOCK CAPITALS) ____________

Card No. ____________

Expires End ____________ Security Code ____________

Gift to CWR

☐ Please send me an acknowledgement of my gift **C** ____________

Gift Aid (your home address required, see overleaf)

giftaid it

I am a UK taxpayer and want CWR to reclaim the tax on all my donations for the four years prior to this year **and on** all donations I make from the date of this Gift Aid declaration until further notice.*

Taxpayer's Full Name (in BLOCK CAPITALS) ____________

Signature ____________ **Date** ____________

* I am a UK taxpayer and understand that if I pay less Income Tax and/or Capital Gains Tax than the amount of Gift Aid claimed on all my donations in that tax year it is my responsibility to pay any difference.

GRAND TOTAL (Total of A, B & C) ____________

Subscriptions by Direct Debit (UK bank account holders only)

One-year subscriptions cost £15.95 (except *Mettle*: £14.50) and include UK delivery. Please tick relevant boxes and fill in the form below.

- ☐ *Every Day with Jesus* (1yr, 6 issues)
- ☐ Large Print *Every Day with Jesus* (1yr, 6 issues)
- ☐ *Inspiring Women Every Day* (1yr, 6 issues)
- ☐ *Life Every Day* (Jeff Lucas) (1yr, 6 issues)
- ☐ *Mettle*: 15–18s (1yr, 3 issues)
- ☐ *YP's*: 11–14s (1yr, 6 issues)
- ☐ *Topz*: 7–11s (1yr, 6 issues)

Issue to commence from

☐ Jan/Feb ☐ Jul/Aug *Mettle* ☐ Jan–Apr

☐ Mar/Apr ☐ Sep/Oct ☐ May–Aug

☐ May/Jun ☐ Nov/Dec ☐ Sep–Dec

CWR Instruction to your Bank or Building Society to pay by Direct Debit

DIRECT Debit

Please fill in the form and send to: CWR, Waverley Abbey House, Waverley Lane, Farnham, Surrey GU9 8EP

Name and full postal address of your Bank or Building Society

To: The Manager ____________ Bank/Building Society

Address ____________

Postcode ____________

Name(s) of Account Holder(s) ____________

Branch Sort Code ____________

Bank/Building Society Account Number ____________

Originator's Identification Number

4	2	0	4	8	7

Reference ____________

Instruction to your Bank or Building Society

Please pay CWR Direct Debits from the account detailed in this Instructio subject to the safeguards assured by the Direct Debit Guarantee. I understand that this Instruction may remain with CWR and, if so, details will be passed electronically to my Bank/Building Society.

Signature(s) ____________

Date ____________

Banks and Building Societies may not accept Direct Debit Instructions for some types of account